BACH TRANSCRIPTIONS

for Piano

TWENTIETH-CENTURY ARRANGEMENTS FROM
CHORAL AND INSTRUMENTAL WORKS

Compiled and edited by
Michael Aston

With an introduction by
David Owen Norris

T0314608

MUSIC DEPARTMENT

OXFORD
UNIVERSITY PRESS

OXFORD
UNIVERSITY PRESS

Great Clarendon Street, Oxford OX2 6DP,
United Kingdom

Oxford University Press is a department of the University of Oxford.
It furthers the University's objective of excellence in research, scholarship,
and education by publishing worldwide. Oxford is a registered trade mark of
Oxford University Press in the UK and in certain other countries

© Oxford University Press 2013

Each contributing party has asserted his/her right under the Copyright, Designs
and Patents Act, 1988, to be identified as the Arranger of his/her Work(s)

Database right Oxford University Press (maker)

First published 2013

All rights reserved. No part of this publication may be reproduced,
stored in a retrieval system, or transmitted, in any form or by any means,
without the prior permission in writing of Oxford University Press

Permission to perform the works in this anthology in public
(except in the course of divine worship) should normally be obtained from
a local performing right licensing organization, unless the owner or the occupier
of the premises being used already holds a licence from such an organization.
Likewise, permission to make and exploit a recording of these works
should be obtained from a local mechanical copyright licensing organization

Enquiries concerning reproduction outside the scope of the above
should be directed to the Music Rights Department, Oxford University Press, at
music.permissions.uk@oup.com or at the address above

ISBN 978-0-19-339261-8

Music and text origination by Katie Johnston
Printed in Great Britain on acid-free paper by
Caligraving Ltd, Thetford, Norfolk.

Contents

Preface

In 1809, the composer Samuel Wesley, who admired Bach so much that he named his son Samuel Sebastian, published transcriptions of the Trio Sonatas for Organ, arranged for three hands at one piano. One would imagine that this was not too exacting a task: as their name implies, the sonatas are in three parts, which would work out at at one part per hand. A work of loving dissemination then, since few English organs of the time had adequate pedal boards. The same idea of wider access lies behind all those nineteenth-century piano duet arrangements of Mozart's string quartets. And yet, already, the particular advantages of the transcription begin to assert themselves. Two pianists can stop and start more easily even than four string players, playing the salient points again and again until the mechanisms of the music's form are deeply absorbed—much more effective than just listening to it as it passes. (The designer Zandra Rhodes always makes her students draw, rather than photograph, when collecting designs in the field. In each case, the willed involvement of the hand ensures understanding.)

Orchestral transcriptions have even more advantages. For those who can't read scores, two staves are better than twenty. And a black and white presentation, shorn of gorgeous orchestral colour, can clarify structural issues. It's a bit like Shakespeare on the radio.

Transcription is a good way to steal a tune too, though Liszt's Schubert Songs, at their best, are co-creations along the lines of 'If only I'd thought of that…', and Rachmaninoff's arrangements of Kreisler are a joyous comparison of virtuosity. Bach is wide open to this sort of larceny: 'Air on the G String', ' Jesu, joy', 'Badinerie', 'Sheep may safely graze'—who wouldn't want to be able to play these melodies?

Even more than his melodies, Bach's chords exert a special power. The harmonic implications of the music for unaccompanied violin or cello have tempted many composers up the primrose path of pinning them down at the piano. Schumann wrote piano accompaniments for the pieces, but other composers have preferred to eliminate the original instrument altogether. Joachim Raff started with the great D minor violin Chaconne in 1865 (expanding it for orchestra and for piano duet in 1873), and by 1875 had polished off most of the solo string music. In 1878 Brahms trumped him with the Chaconne for left hand alone, a clever parallel of limitation. Busoni's two-handed version of 1897 was itself transcribed (still for piano solo) by Alexander Ziloti in 1924.

In 1862, Ignaz Moscheles similarly expanded the melodic and contrapuntal implications of ten preludes from the 'forty-eight' by providing a part for a cello, later expanded to a whole second piano part—a fascinating set of pieces, not at all to be compared with Grieg's second piano parts for Mozart's sonatas. In 1890, Edward MacDowell perhaps too enthusiastically took up the baton in 'Six Little Pieces (after sketches of J. S. Bach)', which amplify pieces that Bach (or in a couple of cases, as we now know, Christian Petzold) thought he had actually finished. MacDowell's work has been replicated in the light of Jacques Loussier by Eduard Pütz in *Let's Swing, Mr. Bach!*, which was probably a good title in 1993. And yet these transcriptions differ only in degree from those that need to work out—to 'realize'—figured basses, where the harmony is indicated by numbers. Granville Bantock's 'Sleepers, Wake' is a remarkable window on late Romantic harmony, all the more because Bantock thought he was restraining himself.

A more reverent attitude to Bach transcription aspires to change not a single note. This is commonly the case in transcriptions of chorale preludes, which were objects of particular devotion. 'So noble, so majestic, so elevated', writes A. M. Henderson in 1911, dedicating his work to Wilhelm Backhaus. 'Full of poetic beauty, rich in fantasy and musical feeling, yet almost unknown', chimes in William Murdoch in 1928, dedicating his selection to Eugene Goossens.

In fact, these dedications are an interesting study. Busoni's Chaconne is dedicated to Eugen d'Albert, another musical polymath, while his E minor Prelude and Fugue is for 'his friend W. H. Dayas', piano professor at the Royal Manchester College of Music. His series of toccatas are dedicated to Robert Freund (the first piano professor at the Zurich Musikschule) with a strong hint that Busoni's transcriptions should form the basis of a High School of Pianoforte Playing. Vivian Langrish dedicated a transcription to his teacher at the Tobias Matthay Piano School, Percy Waller. Cyril Smith, Myra Hess, and Harriet Cohen, assiduous transcribers themselves, were also a good deal dedicated to. (Cohen dedicated one of hers to Henry Hall, and I hope against hope that she meant the famous dance-band leader.)

Behind all this pianism lies the great question of 'playing Bach on the piano'. Surely pianists wanting to play Bach already have an ample supply of suites, toccatas, preludes, and fugues? Here the problem of counterpoint arises. On the piano you can sing out the fugue subject in a way the harpsichord can only dream of. Unfortunately, this manner of playing Bach can eliminate the other musical material completely, reducing the piece to a mere set of repetitions of the subject. Bach composes audibility into the very fabric of his subject, perhaps simply with an ornament, more often with a characteristic interval and articulation. And he could get louder and quieter by manipulating register and texture. It's almost impossible to ignore the piano's dynamic possibilities, but Pandora's box can be locked again by the transcription. Textures can be so arranged, even in frank transcriptions of fugues, that contrapuntal clarity, at least as understood by the arranger, is assured.

In sum, Bach transcriptions allow us to play tunes that belong to someone else, to explore Bach's harmonic mind, to present great music to people who don't like organs (a regrettably large number), and to avoid the technical problems raised by the piano. Above all, they expand our own musical minds by listening to a more or less known phenomenon through someone else's ears.

Publishers all over Europe dabbled in Bach transcriptions, but it was Hubert Foss (1899–1953), the first music editor (1923–1941) at the Oxford University Press and an enthusiastic organizer and conductor of London's Bach Cantata Club, who hit the bullseye by defining a whole era of English music in *A Bach Book for Harriet Cohen*. Originally published in 1932, the Cohen Collection is now made available once again, along with a compilation of single transcriptions published seperately between 1925 and 1954. I welcome them very heartily, all the more because they reflect Foss's vision for amateur music making. When Foss moved on from the OUP Music Department in 1941, Vaughan Williams wrote him a letter, here reproduced by kind permission of Diana Sparkes, Foss's daughter.

> I always admired the way in which you took an interest in even the humblest of music makings—choral competitions school music etc—realizing in profound truth that without the foundation the Elgars & Waltons can't exist.

The uncomprehending few who have criticized these transcriptions for not being like Busoni's miss the point completely. The blurb for Hess's Adagio makes Foss's position crystal clear:

> Every pianist who knows Myra Hess's 'Jesu, Joy of Man's Desiring'—and who does not?—will welcome this more recent BACH adaptation. Try over the opening bars of this exquisite slow piece [the first two bars are printed]. This piece is no more difficult than its world-famous predecessor—if anything, rather easier. It is one of Bach's loveliest flowing melodies and Myra Hess's adaptation is, needless to say, outstanding in its pianistic effect, while faithfully conserving the feeling of the original.

All the pieces in these volumes, even the tricky ones, offer musical rewards to the average pianist as well as to professional artists and their audiences. I suspect we shall hear more of the Bach transcription.

David Owen Norris, 2013

Introduction

The pianist **Myra Hess** (1890–1965) became indelibly associated with Bach after she began playing 'Jesu, joy' by ear in 1920. It was only in 1926 that she was persuaded to write it down and publish it. (Her reluctance may have been connected with Leonard Borwick's transcription of the piece, included in this collection instead of the Hess—see below.) Hess's 'Sleepers, Wake' is a simple treatment of the three-part version from the Schübler publication of the late 1740s, Bach's own reworking of a movement from Cantata No. 140. The acciaccaturas in bars 17 and 20 are masterly touches of voice leading. Her Adagio, from the Toccata, Adagio, and Fugue BWV 564, is slightly more awkward to play, and requires very careful pedalling. Our notions of Baroque style might now lead us to play the third G sharp in bar 3 as a demisemiquaver, but that would be quite foreign to the aesthetic of this transcription.

Edward Krish (d.1976) selected a movement so ripe for transcription that this Siciliano from the Flute Sonata BWV 1031 is one of the most comfortable pieces to play in all of Bach.

The preface by **William Gillies Whittaker** (1876–1944) to his 1929 transcription of Bach's Pastorella BWV 590 runs, in part, as follows:

> While this little work is known to all embryo organists, by virtue of its elementary demands upon independence of hands and feet, it is not heard frequently in public, as players generally prefer to exhibit their skill in pedalling. Moreover, the cessation of the 16ft. tone [the pedal part] after the first movement throws the weight at the beginning instead of at the end. This flaw is not felt in a pianoforte transcription. The various numbers [movements] were generally found singly in old MSS. The title in Forkel's copy is Pastorella. It was altered in the Peters Edition to Pastorale. The original contains no indication of strength, speed or phrasing.

We include two of the four, separate, movements.

Dorothea Salmon's fairly literal transcriptions, with suitable added dynamics, of BWV 729 and 668 were published in 1932. It seems likely that she is the same Dorothea Salmon (1899–1982) who in 1948 wrote a pamphlet, *Jungle Doctor*, about Albert Schweitzer, the Bach specialist. (At her birth, Florence Nightingale wrote to Dorothea's mother, Ellin, to suggest that the baby be called Balaclava.) Salmon's title for BWV 668, 'Wenn wir in höchsten Nöten sein' ('When we are in the greatest need'), is the one Bach used for the version of this melody in the *Orgel-Büchlein*, BWV 641. But, dictating his last piece on his deathbed, Bach apparently was thinking of an even more appropriate hymn sung to the same tune, 'Vor deinen Thron tret ich hiermit' ('I come before Thy throne').

The manuscript, supposedly in the hand of his son-in-law, has that title above the piece.

William H. Harris (1883–1973) was Director of Music at St George's Chapel, Windsor, when his arrangement of 'Bist du bei mir', from the *Clavierbüchlein for Anna Magdalena Bach*, was published in 1949. We now know this to be a song by Gottfried Heinrich Stölzel, but perhaps Bach provided the bass. Harris's enjoyable working-out—'realization'—of the chords is a superb model of its kind, effortlessly treading the tightrope of imagination across the chasm of error.

Gerald M. Cooper (1892–1947) made a great pianistic discovery in the tenor aria from Cantata No. 4 ('Christ lag in Todes Banden'). Bach wrote just for unison violins, voice, and bass, and Cooper finds ingenious ways to manage the texture and even occasionally adds to it. His offering from the *Orgel-Büchlein*, BWV 638 'Es ist das Heil uns kommen her', is note for note, with useful indications as to which hand plays what.

Leonard Borwick (1868–1925) was a pupil of Clara Schumann in Frankfurt, where he also studied composition with Iwan Knorr, the teacher of Roger Quilter, Percy Grainger, Balfour Gardiner, Cyril Scott, and Norman O'Neill—the 'Frankfurt Gang'. Clara Schumann thought him perhaps her finest pupil, and Brahms was impressed by his performance of his D minor Concerto. Borwick frequently accompanied (from memory) the baritone Harry Plunket Greene; he was the favoured accompanist of the violinist Joseph Joachim; and he played duets with Elgar! His transcription of 'Jesu, joy of man's desiring' from Cantata No. 147, published in the year of his death, is simpler and more effective than the famous one by Hess, published the following year. (Make sure that you hold the bass B in bar 15, and similar places, for the whole minim, or the D you add above it on the second crotchet will make nonsense of the harmony.) Borwick's compositional training becomes evident in the haunting suspensions he imagines for bars 19–20 of his transcription of the Sarabande from the Cello Suite BWV 1008.

It's very pleasing that **Hubert J. Foss** (1899–1953) makes an appearance in this selection, not just as a publisher, but as a transcriber too. This mellifluous arrangement of the tenor aria from Cantata No. 85 ('Seht, was die Liebe tut'), with its delicate amplification of Bach's implied dissonances, shows just what a fine ear Foss had, and what a good pianist he was; after all, Walton dedicated his *Three Songs* to Foss and his wife, Dora. They're not easy by any means, and yet the Fosses' recorded performance of them (Walton Gramophone premières,

Dutton Laboratories CDAX 8003) is much more than an interesting historical document. Foss also arranged this aria for two pianos and, much more austerely, for organ.

Harriet Cohen (1895–1967) is chiefly associated with Bach transcriptions through the eponymous OUP collection *A Bach Book for Harriet Cohen* of 1932, but she made some of her own as well. 'Ertödt' uns durch dein' Güte' is the last movement of Cantata No. 22. Cohen ingeniously reduces the four-part choir to a tenor solo. Her transcription of the chorale prelude 'Liebster Jesu, wir sind hier' is a straightforward bit of work with interesting dynamics, dedicated to Mrs Samuel Courtauld, a notable patron of the arts.

Norah Drewett de Kresz (1882–1960) makes a splendid job of the G minor Fugue BWV 578. Look at the way she deals with the long, sustained top A that starts in bar 19, for instance. Her added markings give a better idea than any other

transcription in this collection of the collision between Bach's logic and the Romantic performer's fancy, though the apparently random staccatos in fact have their origin in technical convenience at the 'pedal' entry in bar 17.

Herbert Murrill (1909–1952) moved in the same musical circles as Britten and Auden, working for the Group Theatre Company and the GPO Film Unit. He spent the war, however, decoding enemy signals at Bletchley Park (where he also put on performances of *Dido and Aeneas*). 'Was Gott thut, das ist wohlgethan' is the finale to the first part of Cantata No. 75 and was later reworked by Bach for Cantata No. 100, where two horns begin with their own version of the first bar (consequently adding a bar), going on to decorate the melody with hunting calls. Bach thus shows us a way forward for the transcription—recomposition with organic additions.

David Owen Norris, 2013

Bach Transcriptions for Piano

Wachet auf, ruft uns die Stimme

J. S. BACH
arr. MYRA HESS

© Oxford University Press 1940. This edition © Oxford University Press 2013.

Siciliano
from Sonata in E flat for Flute and Harpsichord

J. S. BACH
arr. EDWARD KRISH

© Oxford University Press 1954. This edition © Oxford University Press 2013.

Pastorella in F major, mov. 3

J. S. BACH
arr. WILLIAM G. WHITTAKER

© Oxford University Press 1929. This edition © Oxford University Press 2013.

In dulci jubilo

J. S. BACH
arr. DOROTHEA SALMON

© Oxford University Press 1932. This edition © Oxford University Press 2013.

Bist du bei mir

J. S. BACH
arr. WILLIAM H. HARRIS

Slow, and gently sustained

© Oxford University Press 1949. This edition © Oxford University Press 2013.

Christ lag in Todes Banden

J. S. BACH
arr. GERALD M. COOPER

© Oxford University Press 1927. This edition © Oxford University Press 2013.

- scen - - - do mol - - - to *ff* marc.

marc.

poco rall.   a tempo

mf

poco rall.

Jesu, bleibet meine Freude

J. S. BACH
arr. LEONARD BORWICK

© Oxford University Press 1925. This edition © Oxford University Press 2013.

Seht, was die Liebe tut

J. S. BACH
arr. HUBERT J. FOSS

© Oxford University Press 1937. This edition © Oxford University Press 2013.

Sarabande
from Cello Suite in D major

J. S. BACH
arr. LEONARD BORWICK

© Oxford University Press 1928. This edition © Oxford University Press 2013.

Ertödt' uns durch dein' Güte

J. S. BACH
arr. HARRIET COHEN

© Oxford University Press 1935. This edition © Oxford University Press 2013.

Cue sized notes are optional.
*If the octave is omitted play

Pastorella in F major, mov. 4

J. S. BACH
arr. WILLIAM G. WHITTAKER

© Oxford University Press 1929. This edition © Oxford University Press 2013.

Liebster Jesu, wir sind hier

J. S. BACH
arr. HARRIET COHEN

© Oxford University Press 1928. This edition © Oxford University Press 2013.

Fugue in G minor

J. S. BACH
arr. NORAH DREWETT DE KRESZ

© Oxford University Press 1936. This edition © Oxford University Press 2013.

Was Gott thut, das ist wohlgethan

J. S. BACH
arr. HERBERT MURRILL

© Oxford University Press 1932. This edition © Oxford University Press 2013.

Adagio

J. S. BACH
arr. MYRA HESS

© Oxford University Press 1937. This edition © Oxford University Press 2013.

Wenn wir in höchsten Nöten sein

J. S. BACH
arr. DOROTHEA SALMON

© Oxford University Press 1932. This edition © Oxford University Press 2013.

Chorale

Chorale

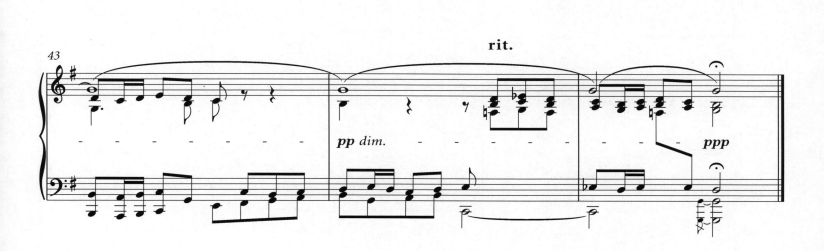

Es ist das Heil uns kommen her

J. S. BACH
arr. GERALD M. COOPER

© Oxford University Press 1927. This edition © Oxford University Press 2013.